I0817400

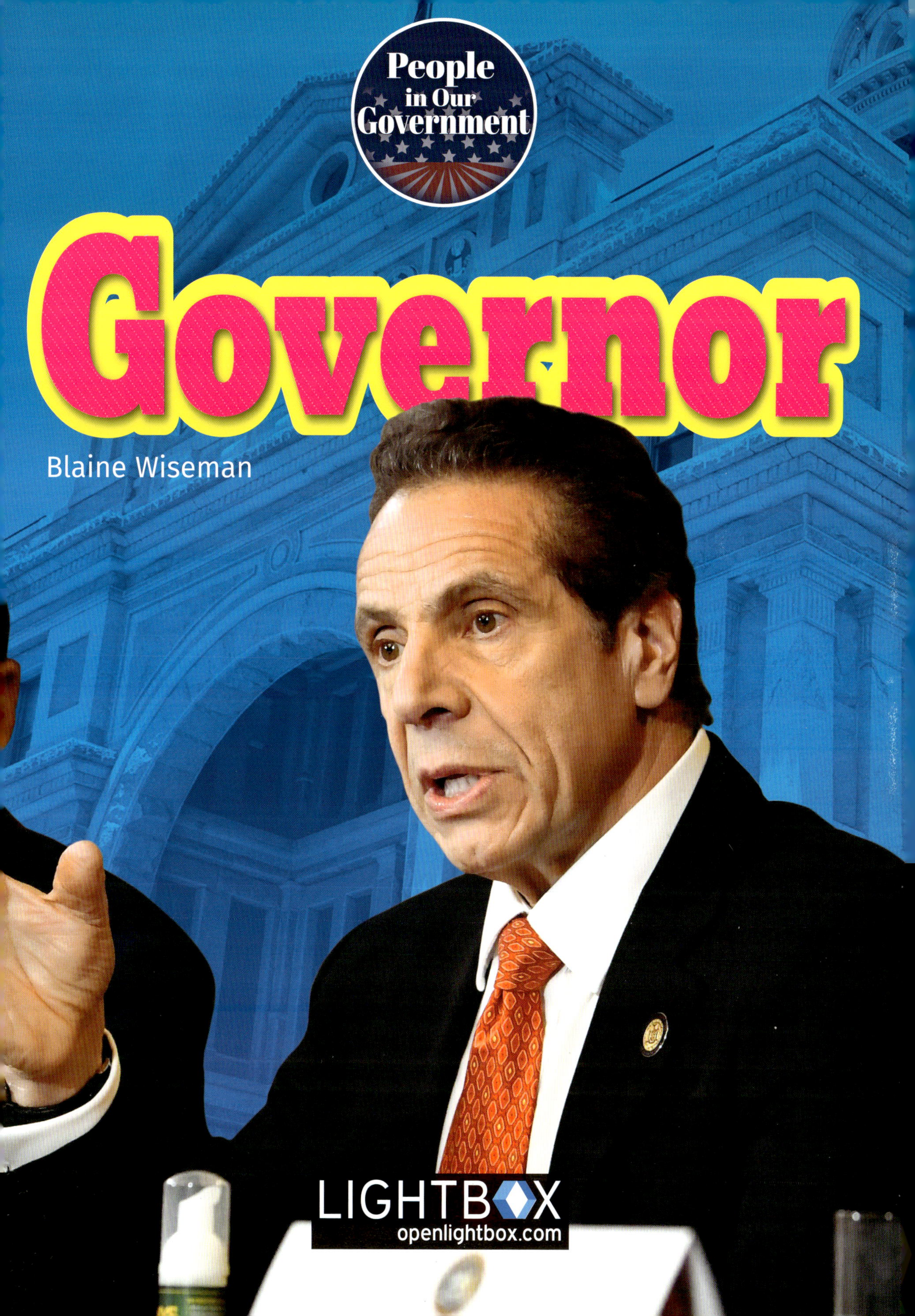
People in Our Government
Governor
Blaine Wiseman
LIGHTBOX
openlightbox.com

Go to
www.openlightbox.com
and enter this book's
unique code.

ACCESS CODE

LBXT3676

Lightbox is an all-inclusive digital solution for the teaching and learning of curriculum topics in an original, groundbreaking way. Lightbox is based on National Curriculum Standards.

STANDARD FEATURES OF LIGHTBOX

AUDIO High-quality narration using text-to-speech system

ACTIVITIES Printable PDFs that can be emailed and graded

SLIDESHOWS Pictorial overviews of key concepts

VIDEOS Embedded high-definition video clips

WEBLINKS Curated links to external, child-safe resources

TRANSPARENCIES Step-by-step layering of maps, diagrams, charts, and timelines

INTERACTIVE MAPS Interactive maps and aerial satellite imagery

QUIZZES Ten multiple choice questions that are automatically graded and emailed for teacher assessment

KEY WORDS Matching key concepts to their definitions

Contents

Who Is the Governor?

A governor is the head of a state in the United States. Each of the 50 states **elects** its own governor. The governor makes important decisions for his or her state, such as which laws should be passed and how to spend the state's money.

The first governor in the United States was Nicholas Cooke. He began as governor of the Rhode Island colony in 1775. Cooke stayed in the role until 1778, two years after the United States won independence from Great Britain.

Nicholas Cooke was Rhode Island's lieutenant governor for two years before becoming governor.

The Government

Each state has its own Constitution. This document establishes the state's government and its laws. The Constitution explains the three branches of state government. Each branch has its own role. Together, they take care of the state and its people.

The legislative branch makes state laws. The executive branch carries out the laws. The judicial branch settles any problems with the laws. The governor is part of the executive branch.

Wisconsin's governor and legislators meet in a building that is more than 100 years old.

Sample Structure of State Government

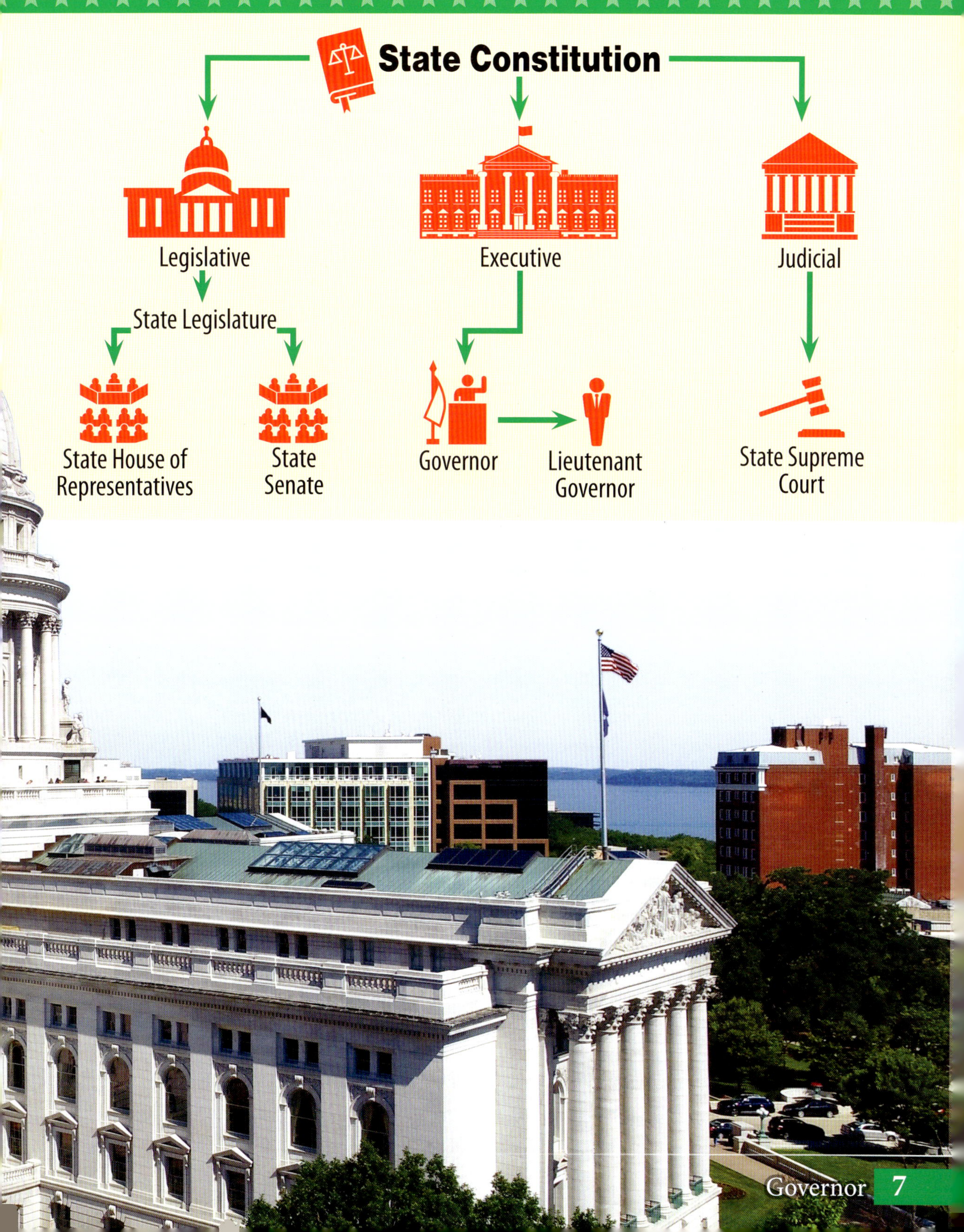

The Role

The role and powers of a governor are found in a state's Constitution. Each state's Constitution is different. This means that each governor has different powers. In most states, the governor **appoints** people to special jobs, such as judges and **cabinet** members.

One of the governor's most important roles is signing **bills**. This is how laws are made. The governor also has the power to decide against new laws. This is called the power of veto. In 2020, the governor of New Mexico used her veto power to cancel projects that would have cost $50 million.

In 2020, Governor Andrew Cuomo of New York appointed people to new jobs to help stop the spread of coronavirus in that state.

New Jersey Governor Chris Christie signed three education bills into law in one day in 2017.

Oregon Governor Kate Brown was born in Spain, but is still a U.S. citizen. Her father was stationed at a U.S. Air Force base there.

What It Takes

A person must meet certain rules in order to become a governor. Different states have different rules. Most say that a governor must be a U.S. **citizen** and at least 30 years old. A person must also live in the state where he or she wants to be governor.

Stevens T. Mason is the youngest governor in U.S. history. Mason was made secretary of the Michigan Territory when he was only 19 years old. He became Michigan's first elected governor at the age of 24. Michigan later changed its law to say that governors must be 30 or older.

Stevens T. Mason was called the "Boy Governor" because of his young age.

Getting the Job

Becoming governor is a long and hard process. Running a **campaign** takes several years, money, and plenty of hard work. There are several steps involved.

1 Each **candidate** fills out paperwork and pays fees to apply to run for office. Candidates also choose which **political party** they want to represent.

2 Candidates **fund-raise**. Money from supporters helps pay for travel, advertising, and campaign posters.

3

Candidates from each party compete against each other in the first round of elections. The winner of this first election becomes his or her party's **nominee**.

4

The nominees travel around the state campaigning. They meet people, talk about their **platform**, and try to win support from voters.

5

Voters cast their vote on Election Day. They vote for the candidate they feel represents their interests. The candidate with the most votes becomes the state governor.

The Capitol

Every state has a capitol building. In most states, it is called the State Capitol. In others, it is called the State House, Statehouse, or Legislative Hall. The Texas State Capitol is in Austin, Texas.

Governor's Public Reception Room
This room is used to host important visitors and special guests to the capitol.

Rotunda
There are 39 state capitol buildings with a domed roof. The rotunda is a central room beneath the dome. Visitors and politicians often gather in the rotunda.

The Texas State Capitol is the **largest** in the country. It has almost **400 rooms**.

In **1977**, the original Arizona State Capitol became a museum. It still houses some government offices.

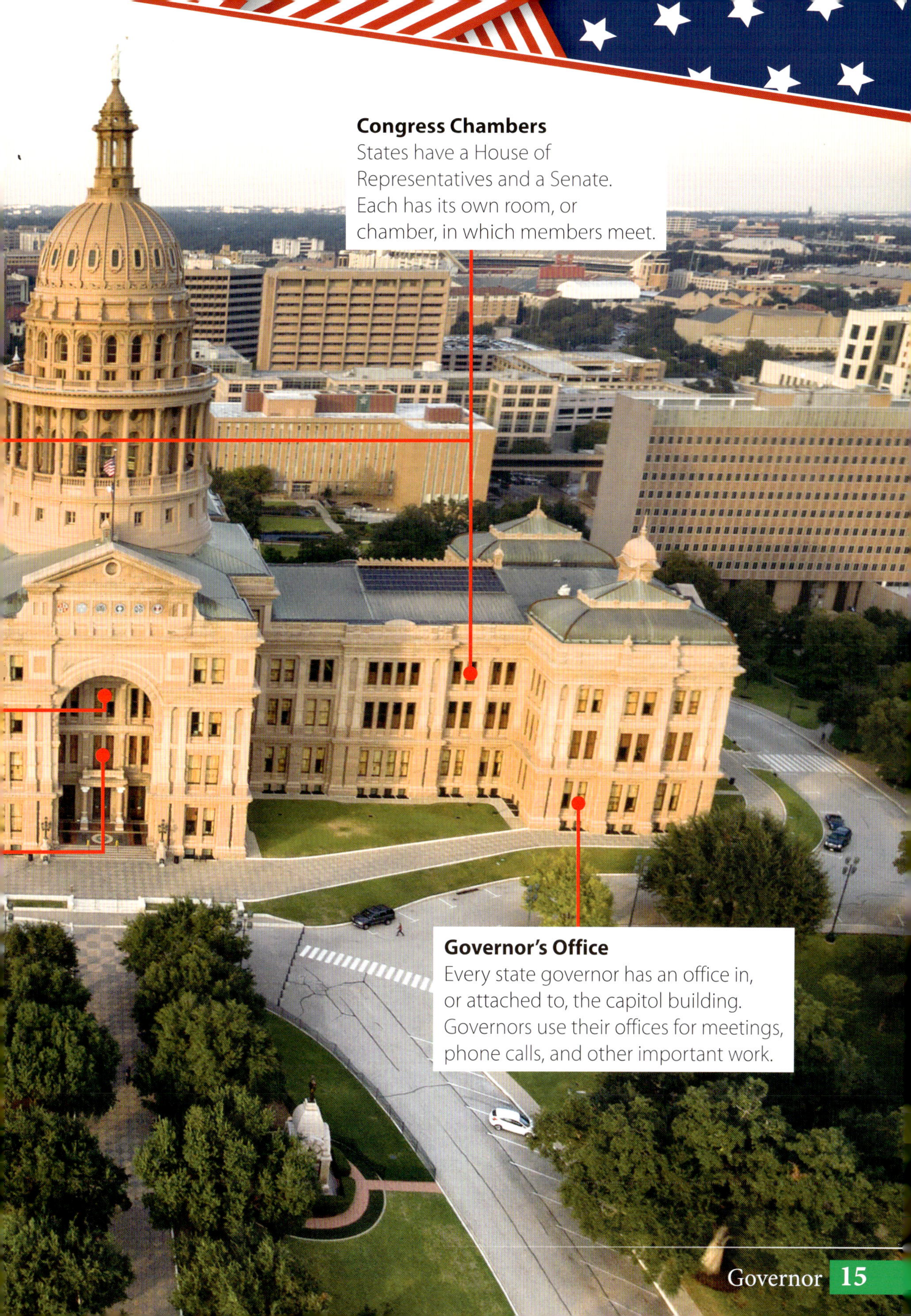
Congress Chambers
States have a House of Representatives and a Senate. Each has its own room, or chamber, in which members meet.
Governor's Office
Every state governor has an office in, or attached to, the capitol building. Governors use their offices for meetings, phone calls, and other important work.

Leading in Public

Part of a governor's job is to keep **constituents** informed about what is happening in the state. He or she must also be willing to listen to the public's concerns. A governor communicates to constituents about new laws and other changes in the state in many different ways.

Most State of the State Addresses are given in January or February.

State of the State Address

Each year, governors give a speech to their state legislature. They talk about what has happened in the state over the last year. They also say what to expect in the coming year.

Town Halls

Governors travel around their states to hold meetings. These meetings take place in town halls, school gyms, libraries, and other public areas. The governor shares ideas and answers questions from the people.

Town halls make it easier for people living in the state to interact with their governor.

Governors sometimes take part in groundbreaking ceremonies for new buildings.

Constituent Visits

Governors celebrate their state's victories and losses with the public. They visit cities and towns for the opening of new public buildings or parks, sports victories, and special achievements. They also respond to disasters in their state.

Constituent Services

It takes a team to keep in touch with thousands of people. The Constituent Services team represents the governor's office and helps the governor by answering phone calls, letters, and emails from the public.

The Constituent Services team is responsible for scheduling the governor for certain events.

A Day in the Life

A governor is always at work. Problems in the state, such as natural disasters, can happen at any time of day or night. The governor must be ready to respond.

A governor is responsible for keeping his or her state's residents informed about changes that may affect them, such as new policies used by state law enforcement.

8:00 am	The governor meets with his or her staff to plan the day.
10:00 am	The governor meets with state senators and representatives. They talk about bills, **taxes**, and issues in the state.
12:00 pm	The governor holds a cabinet meeting. Cabinet members share their departments' concerns and progress.
2:00 pm	The governor travels to another town. On the way, he or she catches up on important paperwork and phone calls.
4:00 pm	The governor attends a ceremony to open a new school in the town.
6:00 pm	The governor attends a town hall meeting. The town's people discuss issues affecting the town and the state.

Notable Governors

Governors are dedicated public servants. Before and after they serve as governor, they often serve in other political positions. Seventeen governors have even gone on to serve as president of the United States.

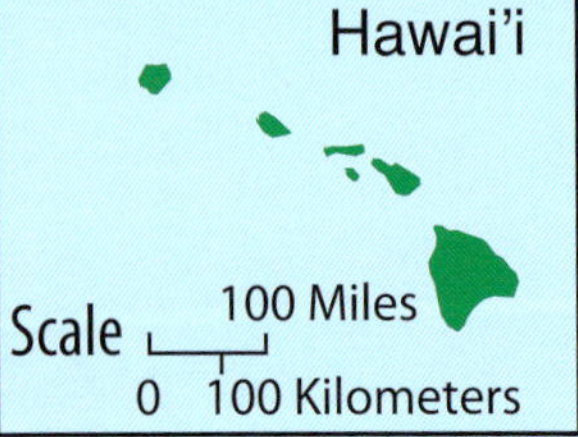

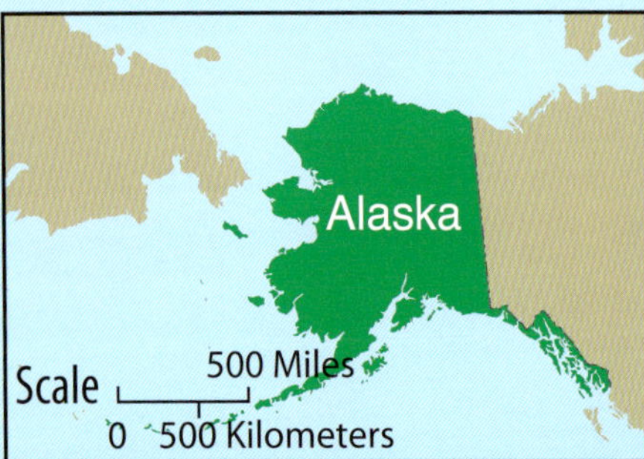

Arnold Schwarzenegger
Years in Office: 2003–2011

Schwarzenegger was born in Austria, but became a U.S. citizen in 1983. Before he became governor of California in 2003, Schwarzenegger was a famous bodybuilder and movie star.

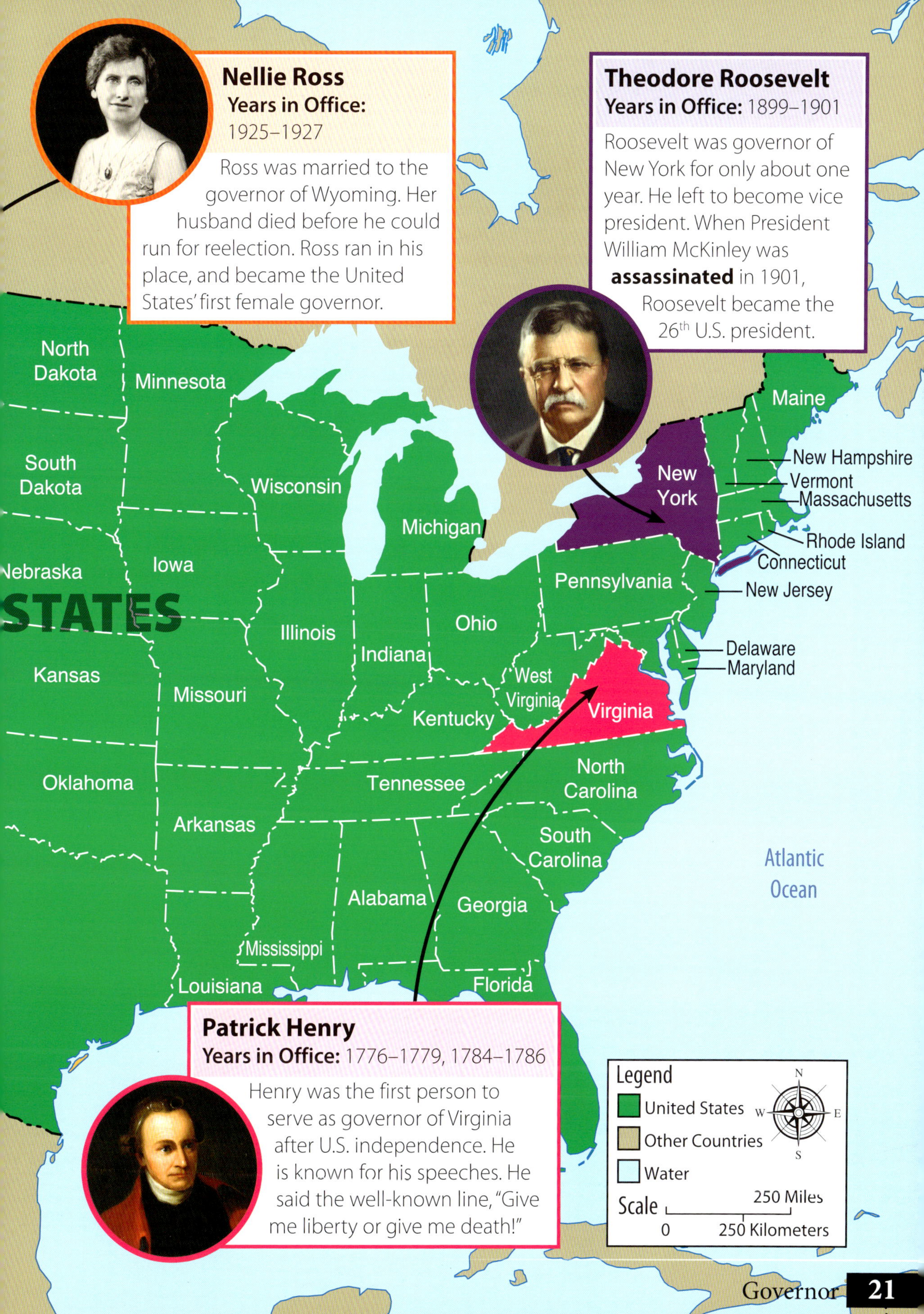

Nellie Ross
Years in Office: 1925–1927

Ross was married to the governor of Wyoming. Her husband died before he could run for reelection. Ross ran in his place, and became the United States' first female governor.

Theodore Roosevelt
Years in Office: 1899–1901

Roosevelt was governor of New York for only about one year. He left to become vice president. When President William McKinley was **assassinated** in 1901, Roosevelt became the 26th U.S. president.

Patrick Henry
Years in Office: 1776–1779, 1784–1786

Henry was the first person to serve as governor of Virginia after U.S. independence. He is known for his speeches. He said the well-known line, "Give me liberty or give me death!"

Quiz

1 Who was the first governor of Rhode Island after the United States won independence from Great Britain?

2 The governor is part of which branch of the state government?

3 Which power lets the governor stop a law from passing?

4 Who is the youngest governor in U.S. history?

5 Which state has the largest capitol building?

6 Who was the first female governor in the United States?

ANSWERS

1 Nicholas Cooke **2** Executive **3** Veto **4** Stevens T. Mason of Michigan **5** Texas **6** Nellie Ross

Key Words

appoints: assigns to a specific job

assassinated: murdered for political reasons

bills: documents proposing new laws

cabinet: a group of people that gives advice to a leader

campaign: an effort to become elected

candidate: a person who seeks or is put forward for a job

citizen: a person who lives in a particular country and legally belongs to that country

constituents: people who live in a politician's area, state, or country

elects: votes into a job

fund-raise: to raise money to support a cause or campaign

nominee: a person who is formally entered as a candidate for political office

platform: a set of goals, ideas, or policies

political party: a group of people who share the same views about the way power should be used in a country

taxes: an amount of money that people pay to the government so that it can pay for public services

Index

LIGHTBOX

SUPPLEMENTARY RESOURCES

Click on the plus icon found in the bottom left corner of each spread to open additional teacher resources.

- Download and print the book's quizzes and activities
- Access curriculum correlations
- Explore additional web applications that enhance the Lightbox experience

LIGHTBOX DIGITAL TITLES

Packed full of integrated media

VIDEOS

INTERACTIVE MAPS

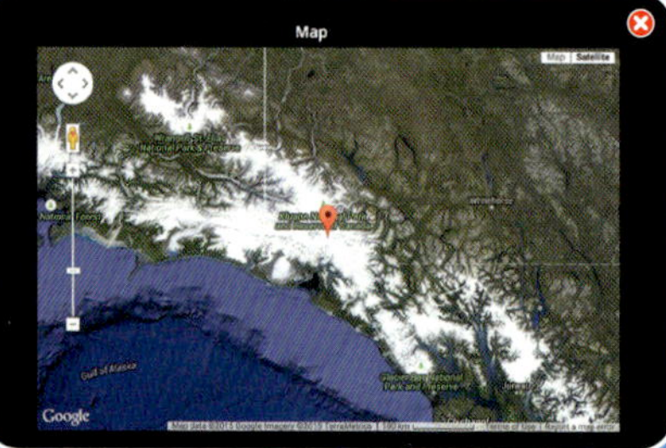

WEBLINKS

SLIDESHOWS

QUIZZES

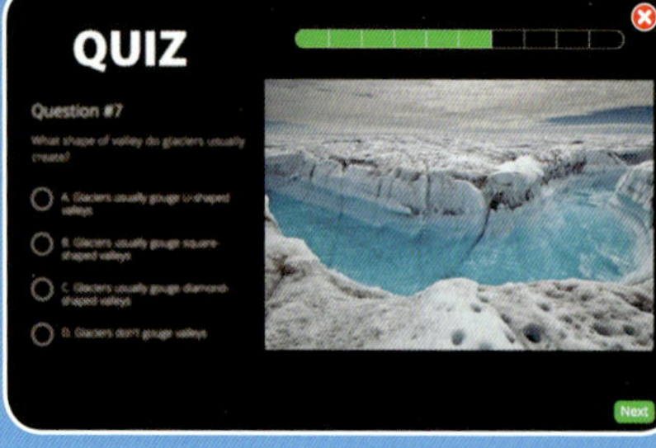

OPTIMIZED FOR

- ✔ TABLETS
- ✔ WHITEBOARDS
- ✔ COMPUTERS
- ✔ AND MUCH MORE!

Published by Smartbook Media Inc.
14 Penn Plaza 9th Floor
New York, NY 10122
Website: www.openlightbox.com

Library of Congress Control Number: 2020938413

ISBN 978-1-5105-5448-1 (hardcover)
ISBN 978-1-5105-5449-8 (multi-user eBook)

Printed in Guangzhou, China
1 2 3 4 5 6 7 8 9 0 24 23 22 21 20

062020
111019

Project Coordinator Heather Kissock
Designer Ana María Vidal

Photo Credits
Every reasonable effort has been made to trace ownership and to obtain permission to reprint copyright material. The publisher would be pleased to have any errors or omissions brought to its attention so that they may be corrected in subsequent printings. The publisher acknowledges Alamy, Getty Images, iStock, and Dreamstime as its primary image suppliers for this title.